T E B H A G A

TEBHAGA

AN ARTIST'S DIARY AND SKETCHBOOK

SOMNATH HORE

TRANSLATED FROM THE BENGALI BY SOMNATH ZUTSHI

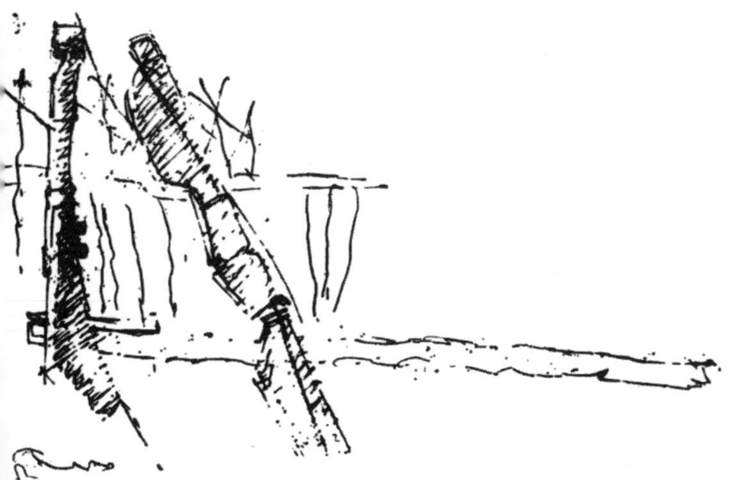

CALCUTTA 2009

First published in 1989
This edition published in 2009
Second printing 2022

ISBN 978 81 7046 078 7

Book and cover design by Sunandini Banerjee, Seagull Books, Calcutta
Printed and bound by Hyam Enterprises, Calcutta, India

Preface

Immediately after my *Tebhaga Diary* appeared in *Ekshan*, Samik Bandyopadhyay proposed bringing out an English translation of the work. (Subarnarekha has since taken the responsibility of publishing the original Bengali text.) I was quite sure that Naveen Kishore of Seagull Books and Samik had made the proposal not in the hope of financial gain but out of love of the subject. I was at the time so busy with my work that to worry about writing seemed like apostasy, which is why I did not show much interest then. Now it no longer seems such an insuperable obstacle. Moreover, they are prepared to give the series of sketches in the diary the value they deserve. A costly proposition and a tempting offer! These sketches were made when I was in my second year as a student at the Government Art College in Calcutta. One should not expect any artistic skill from them. Still, even today, my attachment to these drawings remains strong.

Somnath Zutshi, like a younger brother to me, has translated this diary into English. Samik Bandyopadhyay has taken the responsibility of writing the introduction. An account of the Tebhaga revolt, which made manifest the peasant's hunger for land at a crucial phase of the freedom struggle and led to bloodshed and violence, emerges in Samik's contribution.

I am deeply indebted to Naveen Kishore, Somnath Zutshi and Samik Bandyopadhyay. I am also especially grateful to Nirmalya Acharya, the editor of *Ekshan*, without whose constant persuasion this diary would never have appeared in print.

SOMNATH HORE
Santiniketan, 26 July 1989

Introduction

D. N. Dhangare describes the Tebhaga movement in Bengal in 1946–47 as 'the outgrowth of left-wing mobilization of the rural masses, . . . the first *consciously* attempted revolt by a politicized peasantry in Indian history'. He defines its scope in terms of 'a struggle by sharecroppers to retain a two-thirds share of the produce for themselves and thereby to reduce the rent they paid to jotedars—a class of rich farmers who held superior rights in land—from one-half to one-third of their produce' (*Peasant Movements in India,1920–50*, Delhi: 1983, p. 155). Behind that bland account of the revolt lies a long history of exploitation that had evolved out of the Permanent Settlement of 1793 as subinfeudation and continuous fragmentation had eaten into the power of the original zamindars, 'the proprietors of the soil', who came to lease out their estates to the jotedars, intermediary tenure-holders. They in their turn sublet their plots to bargadars, the actual cultivators who provided seeds, cattle, agricultural implements and manure, had no permanent right to reap the same plot every year, and paid the jotedar a produce rent of half the harvest for this 'privilege'. The bargadars were described in different terms in different parts of the undivided State of Bengal. In northern Bengal, the more common term was *adhiar* (from *adhi*, a half share). Elsewhere they were *bhagchashis* (literally, sharecroppers). The injustice implicit in the system that served to widen the divide between the non-cultivating landlord and the actual tiller of the soil was quite apparent. But the system had created its own defence in the massive phenomenon of rural indebtedness, With the jotedar himself almost always doubling as the moneylender and thus holding the small-holders and the bargadars in his grip.

Even before the political radicalization of Bengal in the 1920s could turn to land relations, communalism reared its ugly head in 1925–27, curbing the possibilities of a concerted movement by or for a growing poor peasant-sharecropper-agricultural labour class ruthlessly exploited by a rich peasant-moneylender-trader class. The Land Revenue Commission, 1938, appointed under Fazlul Haque's popular government in Bengal, studied the agrarian situation in the state, and recommended that the bargadars be treated as 'protected tenants', and that 'the share of the crop, legally recoverable from them, be reduced from half to one-third of the produce'. Haque's coalition government failed to act upon the recommendation, and earned the ire of the Krishak Praja Party, Haque's own party, whose radical section described the ministry as 'subservient to British Imperialism and Bengal Landlordism'. Yet this first official acknowledgement of the injustice, and suggestion of a fair remedy, lay behind the sharpening of the agrarian class struggle under the leadership and initiative of the Communist Party which had just emerged on the scene.

The Tebhaga movement led by Communist workers had to maintain a firm resistance to communal tendencies lest they tear into the solidarity of the increasingly impoverished mass of sharecroppers. The Communist leaders of the movement represented a mix of locals and outsiders who had settled into the more militant pockets, several of these outsiders being drawn from the revolutionaries released from the state prisons in 1937–38. Detained for their involvement in the terrorist movements, many of them had accepted Marxism in prison, and on their release went out to the villages to work among the peasantry and set up units of the Kisan Sabha. the national union of the peasants which had, by then, come under the control of the Communists. Against the background of the communal riots of 1946, the Bengal Provincial Kisan Sabha gave the call for the Tebhaga movement in September 1946. Partha Chatterjee offers the finding: 'Despite the presence of Communist workers, the tebhaga movement did not get off the ground in Barddhaman or Medinipur (except briefly in the Nandigram area of Tamluk), but became a powerful movement in these areas of northern Bengal and in the Sundarban region of southern Bengal where sharecropping was a widespread historical form of subtenancy with inferior rights' (*Bengal 1920–47: The Land Question*, Calcutta: 1984, p. 203).

When the Tebhaga struggle began in November 1946, the communal riots had just subsided in Bengal, but the tension remained: Somnath Hore, the young artist, felt it, 'on the stifling Calcutta night of 17 December 1946', boarding 'a third class compartment of the North Bengal Express' on his way to Rangpur in north Bengal. In his prefatory note to the first publication of his *Tebhaga Diary* in the original Bengali in *Ekshan* (annual number, 1981), Hore recalled: 'December 1946. I was a student in the second year at the Calcutta Government Art School. The revered Somnath Lahiri and Nripen Chakrabarty told me, "If you want to have a look at the Tebhaga movement, go to Rangpur." '

Hore's diary covers only 12 days and bears the mark of a young radical watching and admiring the revolutionary fervour and solidarity of a peasantry that he had never really seen from so close before. Nowhere in his account is there any premonition of the rapid break-up of the movement under what Partha Chatterjee describes as 'direct and massive state repression, supported by the armed strength of the jotedar class' (ibid. p. 206). In a more objective account of the Tebhaga movement in Rangpur, Sunil Sen, the activist historian of the struggle, wrote:

> In Rangpur the movement remained confined to Nilphamari subdivision which was severely hit by the great famine of 1943. As in Thakurgaon the bargadars, mainly Rajbanshi and Muslim, were concentrated in this subdivision. Within a month

> the movement spread to six police stations—the leadership was taken by Mohi Bagchi, Mani Krishna Sen and Mantu Majumdar, who went underground to evade arrest and guide the movement. Hundreds of volunteers went to the field and removed the crop to the bargadar's *khamar* [threshing floor]. In the second week there was a clash. Some Muslim jotedars of Dimla, armed with guns, raided the house of a bargadar to snatch away the crop. The peasants, led by Bachcha Muhammad and Tatnarayan Ray, resisted the attack; the jotedars fired on the peasants; Tatnarayan was killed and Bachcha severely wounded. The news of Tatnarayan's death spread like wildfire and about 3,000 peasants, armed with lathis and spears, assembled in the village. Since the jotedar was a Muslim, the leaders persuaded the peasants, who were in a militant mood, not to attack his house; they were afraid that an attack on a Muslim jotedar could spark off a communal riot. The peasants put the jotedar under social boycott and held a demonstration that marched through the villages to Nilphamari town. The jotedars fled the village and bided their time (*Agrarian Struggle in Bengal 1946-47*, New Delhi: 1972, p. 40).

Continuing his history for the whole state, Sen records:

> By the middle of December the agrarian struggle had spread to eleven districts and lakhs of bargadars had carried crop to their *khamars*. It was a partial victory; since the paddy was stacked in their *khamars* the jotedars could no longer deprive them of their share by force of fraud or both . . . Meanwhile repression had been let loose on the peasants. On 4 January 1947 the police opened fire on a peasant demonstration in Talpukur village in Chirirbandar in Dinajpur district, killing Sibram, a Santal landless peasant, and Samiruddin, also a landless peasant, on the spot . . . Several peasants received bullet injuries . . . On the morrow of the Chirirbandar firing Fazlur Rahman, land revenue minister, announced in a public meeting at Serajgunj that the Bengal government would soon bring a bill to present eviction of bargadars and make provision for them to get a two-thirds share, jotedars getting one-third. The Bengal Bargadars Temporary Regulation Bill was published in the *Calcutta Gazette* on 22 January 1947 (ibid., pp. 44–7).

It soon became clear:

> that the government was not serious about passing the Bargadars Bill, but had embarked on a repressive policy . . . The spontaneous phase of the movement was over. In face of police repression the peasants, particularly Muslim peasants,

> were showing signs of vacillation. Only the Hajongs and Santals remained as militant as ever, but they comprised a small section of the rural population . . . In its meeting held in the second week of January 1947 the Provincial Kisan Council admitted its failure to work out 'the forms of struggle' . . . In the third week of February police repression began in full swing, and the government made it clear that the object was a knock-out blow (ibid., pp. 61–3).

Sen ends his account on a note of bitterness, with the observation that 'agrarian unrest appeared to be the only obstacle in the path of the peaceful transfer of power'. Hence the movement was dropped rather unceremoniously. Nothing of that sordid story surfaces in Hore's account, for in that moment of glory there was no way one could see the more insidious moves underground.

In the early 1940s, with the international struggle against fascism shaping a radical camaraderie among writers and artists all over the world, the Communist Party in India showed a genuine interest in forging connections between writers and artists and peasant and working-class insurgency. One can trace the roots of this process of radical conscienciza-tion of the artist back to the 1920s in Germany when Georg Grosz wrote:

> What should you do to give content to your paintings?

> Go to a proletarian meeting; look and listen how people there, people just like you, discuss some small improvement of their lot.
>
> And understand—these masses are the ones who are reorganizing the world. Not you! But you can work with them. You could help them if you wanted to! And that way you could learn to give your art a content which was supported by the revolutionary ideals of the workers ('On My Next Paintings', in Dore Ashton (ed.), *Twentieth Century Artists on Art,* New York: 1985, p. 64).

Both in his writing and sketches, Hore has the same approach to the Tebhaga experience. He documents the movement, without any attempt to abstract or distort. In his text he captures some of the most striking features of the mobilization, also noticed by other observers. Sunil Sen quotes a *Statesman* special correspondent who, like Hore, saw power and self-confidence in the lathi:

> Dumb through past centuries, he is today transformed by the shout of a slogan. It is inspiring to see him marching across a field with his fellows, each man shouldering a lathi like a rifle, with a red flag at the head of the procession. It is sinister to hear them greet each other in the silence of bamboo groves with clenched left fists raised to foreheads and a whispered 'Inquilab, comrade'.

CHITTAPRASAD, TEBHAGA

DEBABRATA MUKHOPADHYAY, TEBHAGA

The carrying of lathis is apparently compulsory. 'The party requires that we carry the Red Flag and lathis', one peasant who looked like an aboriginal told me. 'It is a sign of our solidarity.' . . . a townsman sympathizer declared, 'To people who have been downtrodden for generations the lathi gives courage' (Sen, *Agrarian Struggle*, p. 38).

In his drawings, Hore uses lines in an impersonal, photographic way to construct volume, and reveal personalities in the faces. There is more conscious style in the Tebhaga works of his contemporaries, Chittaprasad (1915–78) and Debabrata Mukhopadhyay (b. 1918), reproduced on the previous page. While Chittaprasad uses mass and weight to convey the strength of the fighting peasants, Mukhopadhyay chooses the rhythm of sinuous line for the same purpose. They load their images with meanings. Hore stands apart, in his cool objectivity, in his uncompromising commitment to the immediate truth of the experience. His subsequent treatment of the Tebhaga theme about six years later is marked by a different outlook, for by now Hore has a more historical view of the movement, already a thing of the past politically; and a different approach to art after having come into contact with Benodebihari Mukherjee in Santiniketan.

Between 1946 and the early 50s, when he did the wood engravings reproduced in this book, the political history of Bengal had undergone a series of convulsions. The Communist Party, Hore's party, stood by Nehru's Congress to see that the transfer of power came through smoothly. Then, soon after, it called for revolt against the new government, was banned and faced the worst kind of state repression, compelling it to go underground. It surfaced again before the first general elections in 1951, to emerge as the parliamentary opposition. It was a period of police firings on peasants, workers and the middle class alike, firings even in prison, where hundreds languished without trial. Hore himself had gone undergound. And Hore was one of those who dropped out when the Party wrote off the mobilization of the late 1940s and settled down to official politics. Chittaprasad, best known for his inspiring celebratory panels on the people's movements of the period, carried regularly by the Party periodicals, withdrew into a strange, indifferent isolation, the 'massiveness' and the large eyes so prominent in his works somehow going back to their source in the benign decorativeness of the *pats*. Mukhopadhyay, the most bohemian and individualistic of the three, refused to be concerned with the Party's politics as such; he retained his commitment to the ultimate cause of Communism and went on serving it unquestioningly, developing his linear rhythms to greater freedom and dynamism.

Hore himself had to withdraw from the art school and go underground as a Party activist in 1949. When he came out in the open, he sought for fresh artistic inspiration, and met Benodebihari, 'who awakened him to the necessity of recognizing the vital role of pictorial space in any composition, and of the necessity of not treating the pictorial space as representing the natural space. This bit of advice proved of seminal consequence later in his works' (Pranabranjan Ray, *Somnath Hore*, New Delhi: n.d., p. 4).

With his greater interest in both space and material, Hore took a fresh look at the Tebhaga experience in his wood engravings of the early 1950s. His images were now more visionary: the negotiation/confrontation with wood, which necessitated a more active participation in the creative process than that required by ink on paper, demanded greater penetration into the experience itself. The wood engravings, especially the ones reproduced in this book on pages 31 and 53, give meaning to the movement that had remained unfinished and been abandoned. For, what the sharper opposition of black and white in these pictures underscores is a kind of illumination, a light glowing on the faces, chiselling them out of the darkness. Both are pictures of meetings, some of which have already been documented in the diary in their more immediate reality. But now Hore brings to the experience of the night meetings the glow of awareness and faith that blazed in the villages he visited in 1946. Unlike Chittaprasad, who gave it all up from a sense of betrayal, Hore persisted with a dogged determination in his penetration of a reality which he defines in terms of man's inhumanity to man, power riding roughshod over people, leaving them destitute and broken, with no fresh mobilization in sight. To penetrate into that reality, Hore set up for himself the barriers of material which he had to break into (like wood at first, and then paper pulp for his first 'wounds') or mould, as with bronze (which is now his material—for his new 'Wounds'). Hore's vision of wounds bears within it the experience of the Tebhaga movement and the way it has receded into the past and memory, leaving only the impression of an enormous wound, a wound created by a kind of betrayal, which was not just political but moral in the deepest sense. Hore has travelled a long way from those early, sunny sketches of a rural community in its first flush of a sense of power and achievement; to his darker evocations of the same experience, now already irretrievably lost, in the wood engravings; to the white paper pierced with a knife or the metal with gaping wounds in all their pain and horror.

When Hore first showed me the diary, and I suggested that it be printed as a book, I could sense the 'weakness' he had for these sketches of the Tebhaga. He speaks of the 'weakness' in his *Ekshan* note. 'Weakness' is a word that means a lot in this context. For it carries also the feeling of weakness that a sensitive artist bears within him when he withdraws in pain and grief and with a sense of helplessness from militancy in the cause of suffering humanity.

Writing this piece when the book is set up and almost ready, I have a sense of pride in having been associated with the making of this book, the diary translated with the original sketches, and the late works—the wood engravings—that grew out of them. Debabrata Mukhopadhyay, who still takes pride in being a Communist artist and carries warm memories of his Tebhaga experiences, was kind enough to give me access to his Tebhaga work, reproduced here. Smaran Ghoshal, nephew of Chittaprasad, and an art lover, gave us access to the Chittaprsad work. This piece should close with thanks to both of them.

Samik Bandyopadhyay
Calcutta 1990

TEBHAGA

'IT WAS A BEAUTIFUL SIGHT.' 25 DECEMBER 1946.

A BHUTIYA
ON THE TRAIN.
18 DECEMBER 1946.

Tuesday, 17 December 1946

On the stifling Calcutta night of 17 December 1946, I found shelter in a Third Class compartment of the North Bengal Express. When I woke from my exhausted sleep on the morning of the 18th, I saw spread out before me a vast expanse of open fields, scattered with patches of golden paddy, the dew on them glistening in the morning sun. The occasional tiny villages were a dense green, with straggling cottages, some sturdy still, some crumbling. It was early enough for people to have just woken up. Some were sitting out smoking their hookahs, others looking for odd jobs, their oxen tethered to an open stall and a pile of recently harvested paddy heaped in a corner of the courtyard.

It was nearly eight o'clock when I got off at Parbatipur to change trains. After a cup of tea, I got on the Rangpur train. Having found a seat, I sketched a Bhutiya who was on his way back to Rangpur from Calcutta. He had on a grimy shirt over a pair of tight pyjamas, a grimy jacket and an equally grimy cap; and he sported the inevitable kukri at his waist. Comrade Kamaniya said, 'They work as gatekeepers for the local Marwari jotedars. A cunning lot.'

WHERE'S THE OPEN FIELD, THE WIDE ROAD . . . WHERE'S THE SHADE, MY FRIEND, WHERE'S THE WATER?

A PETTY BLACKMARKE-
TEER AT PARBATIPUR.
18 DECEMBER 1946.

As the train pulled out, my eye was drawn to the vista outside: the fields a mingling of reds and blues, the trees a vivid green and the houses white or reddish. These were interspersed with strips of dazzling mustard fields. It was a beautiful sight.

Wrapped in white and working together in groups of five to seven, men were harvesting rice on this winter morning. There was a black cow somewhere, a white goat elsewhere. Everyone was out with daybreak in search of food.

All of a sudden, I noticed a rice mill. These have been set up by Marwaris from outside Bengal and have apparently spread all over north Bengal. The Marwari traders buy paddy cheap to sell the rice dear. The smoke-begrimed brick ribs of the structure were an eyesore in the midst of all the greenery, a bitter taste amidst the plenty nature had to offer.

I arrived at Rangpur at about ten o'clock. Keshto-da, Ramen Banerjee and Sudhir Mukherjee were there to meet me. There are two means of transport in Rangpur—cycle-rickshaws and horse-drawn carriages. The rates are normally four annas per head for a

TWO MARWARI BROTHERS AT RANGPUR STATION.
18 DECEMBER 1946.

A VOLUNTEER.
23 DECEMBER 1946.

A CHARECROPPER VILLAGE. 19 DECEMBER 1946.

rickshaw, three annas per head on a horse-cart—but rise automatically as soon as they spot a stranger. The Party office at Rangpur looks passable from the outside; the Party bookstall is beautiful and the commune not bad. The food at the commune is fairly simple.

In the afternoon, on the way to Domar, I met Rupnarayan, the comrade from Dinajpur, who told me heroic tales about the Tebhaga movement. The police had gone to a village in Rampur to put up a show of strength against the peasants. In the process, they got a proper hammering from the peasant women. Some policemen had their limbs broken, whilst others had broken rifle butts. A few of the women received minor injuries. The jotedars were failing to check the spread of the movement in spite of their concerted efforts.

In another village, the jotedars met secretly. One of them proposed that Rupnarayan and Kali be kidnapped. A barber who was shaving one of them spoke up: 'Why don't you first see if you can touch them, babu, before trying to kill them!' A lawyer present at the meeting then explained that having them killed off was no easy matter. These men were giving shape to the peasants' cherished desires. If they were kidnapped or killed, the peasants would explode in a frenzy in all the villages at once, and the situation would simply go from bad to worse.

In yet another village, the jotedars paid out of their own pockets for a police encampment to terrorize the peasants, who, however, continued unconcernedly harvesting the rice in organized bands. Since the police didn't seem to have the nerve to prevent this, the landlords grew despondent. They realized what a waste it was to support the police. They asked the policemen to strike camp and came to an agreement with the peasants. Rupnarayan said, 'The peasants are organized in the villages. They are saying, "We will harvest the crop and store it ourselves, and give the landlord his share. He'll have to accept what we allot him. And should his thugs or the police turn up, we'll face them and not show our backs." '

I went to the Domar Krishak Samiti (Peasants' Association) office at night, and met Abani Bagchi. I heard reports from him about the Tebhaga movement in Domar and Dimla. The rice harvesting was being done in a scattered and desultory manner and not on a wide scale. But it was to start in earnest in a day or two. The people were gathering under the red flag.

Some members of a Krishak Samiti from a particular village were calling on people to the beating of drums in the marketplace, asking them to gather for a meeting to discuss the Tebhaga issue. A number of jotedars gathered and prevented them from beating their drums. That was on a Saturday. The peasants met and resolved to boycott the weekly market the following Tuesday, 17 December. And that was exactly what had happened—a total strike. I even heard about the boycott from the women of Badgachha. They called it a *hat hartal* (market strike).

The *hat hartal* gave Khoka Thakur, one of the aforementioned joetdars, a real scare. He apparently told the farmers, 'I am sorry I misbehaved. I'll make a public apology.'

In another village, the jotedar attempted to grab a peasant's land. A few hundred volunteers promptly gathered and chased the jotedar and his hired men away.

Most of the stories were similar. The reports also gave me an inkling of the mischief caused by the local Congress and Muslim League activists: Tebhaga was a Communist provocation, the land was going to be distributed to the peasants anyway, harvesting the rice by force would mean police intervention and baton charges, there would be communal riots, and so on. These were the ideas that they were spreading. And, of course, the middle classes were wholeheartedly agreeing with them. But the peasants were paying them no heed whatsoever, saying instead, 'If the Hindu and the Muslim jotedars seem able to gang up so effectively, we Hindu and Muslim peasants can stand together as well.'

I had dinner with a comrade. Very simple fare—rice, dal and a vegetable curry of potato, radish and brinjal. I hadn't had much sleep the previous night. Fell asleep early from sheer exhaustion.

Thursday, 19 December 1946

I set out around half-past nine in the morning after breakfast, to visit one of the centres of the Tebhaga movement. Prior to this, I had only heard about it from various comrades, and read about it in the papers. We, that is, Keshto-da, Ramen Banerjee, Ghulam Aziz and I were going to Badgachha. A little beyond Domar station, a farmer called out to Ghulam Aziz, 'Comrade, we're for Tebhaga.' There were three or four of them, harvesting rice on their own land. Aziz shouted back, 'You're growing rice on your own land, through your own hard work. It's not Tebhaga for you, it's one hundred per cent. What on earth would you be doing Tebhaga for? That's only for those who make fortunes by exploiting the labour of others and squeeze the peasant's land dry. They'll have to accept Tebhaga.' The farmers nodded in agreement. 'You're right brother. Carry on with Tebhaga.'

We chatted with a few peasants as we entered Badgachha village, but their response was rather depressing. They seemed quite unenthusiastic about the rice harvest. We were here because we had heard that the rice harvesting had started in this village. Yet it seemed as though these people knew nothing about it. But we soon perked up as we went further. Two peasant women talked to us and said, 'We did some harvesting yesterday. The comrades are on the other side of the village.' The women were very enthusiastic. With real warmth they directed us to the red flag camp and seemed very pleased to hear that we were part of the Tebhaga movement.

Some lads working in a tobacco field answered Ghulam Aziz's questions with great eagerness, saying that they dared the jotedars to do their worst. Tebhaga was what they believed in; they intended to

WORKING IN THE TOBACCO FIELD.
19 DECEMBER 1946.

তামাকের ক্ষেত 19.12.

RUPKANTA-DA.
21 DECEMBER 1946.

complete harvesting the rice the next day. Their excited conversation was all about when they would get to the field all together, the slogans they would shout and how they would store the paddy in their own granaries once the harvesting was done.

Finally, we got to the camp. Comrade Narayan Banerjee was busy discussing the rice harvesting programme with some farmers. They greeted us with a red salute. We answered in kind. Everyone was saying the same thing, 'We want Tebhaga. No one's afraid of the jotedars. They've lost their nerve after the *hat hartal*. Khoka Thakur, the one who tried to stop the drumming in the market-place, has said that he is going to agree to our demands.'

MOHAN-DA.
20 DECEMBER 1946.

Rupkanta-da, a local peasant leader, Mohan-da and Comrade Panchu turned up. It was decided to call a closed meeting that night. We expressed doubts—would there be a large enough gathering as such short notice? Rupkanta-da said, 'Don't worry about it. Once people hear that Tebhaga leaders from Calcutta have arrived, they won't be able to stay away.'

THE TOBACCO FIELD.
19 DECEMBER 1946.

I wandered off, notebook and pen in hand. Men of all ages, from children to grandfathers, were working in the tobacco fields, clad in the briefest of loin-cloths. Women wrapped from chest to knee were grazing their cows. They were not a well-built people, neither the men nor the women. One look could tell that they worked very hard for very little to eat. Their huts were small and built of mud and straw; they had cows for ploughing but these were thin and scrawny. I saw no other domestic animals apart from a few stray goats; certainly no ducks, hens or pigeons.

DINESH-DA.
21 DECEMBER 1946.

I returned for a bath and a quick meal. Rice, dal, and, through the kindness of a peasant comrade who had caught it, some fish. Dinesh Lahiri arrived in the evening. In Rangpur I had been told that Dinesh-da was the local gazette. He told me a lot of things about local customs and conditions, including *kain*. This is a custom prevalent among the local sharecroppers. A sharecropper who becomes a *dena* or widower faces a lot of difficulties and has problems raising a family, cultivating his land and running a household. If he is lucky enough to fall in love with a widow, he has a way out. If both are agreeable, they can live together as man and wife in his house. This sort of marriage is known locally as *kain*. Unfortunately, there's one rather serious drawback. The children born of such relationships are considered illegitimate, and therefore have no status in local society.

A JOTEDAR

The jotedars have thousands of crafty tricks for exploiting the peasants. For instance, when they loan grain to a peasant, they use a small scoop called a *done* with which they dole out the rice. But when the peasant comes to repay the debt of paddy, the jotedar invariably uses a larger scoop. Should the peasant enquire about the previous

A PLOUGH.
26 DECEMBER 1946.

scoop, pat comes the reply, 'God only knows what the kids have done with it.'

In one village, some Muslim jotedars decided to try and start a communal riot between the Hindu and Muslim sharecroppers. They told the Mulsims, 'If you stop the Hindus from harvesting the rice, we'll give you extra shares.' The Muslims said, 'Sorry, we'll have nothing to do with it.' The irate jotedars next went to a local fair and told the Muslim traders, 'We'll burn your houses down. But don't worry, we'll compensate you for your losses; all you have to do is say that the Hindus did it.' The traders retorted with folded hands, 'Please don't involve us in all this, we're not interested. And if you pressurize us we'll move out at once with our stalls and everything.' The frustrated jotedars finally got the message—they decided to seek a compromise with the peasants.

KESHTO-DA.
19 DECEMBER 1946.

The meeting took place as scheduled at night, under the open sky, on the straw laid out on the ground inside the roofless shed of a sharecropper. Keshto-da was the principal speaker. The meeting started at about half-past nine, with close to 200 sharecroppers and peasants attending. Some of them had walked more than two miles on a bitterly cold winter's evening in order to take part.

A PARTICIPANT AT THE NIGHT MEETING.
19 DECEMBER 1946.

A PEASANT LEADER SPEAKS AT THE MEETING. 19 DECEMBER 1946.

Keshto-da spoke about harvesting the rice. 'You must finish harvesting the rice. Don't wait for the others. Just organize yourselves into groups and start. You mustn't store the harvested grain in the jotedar's shed. Keep it in your homes and then distribute it according to the Tebhaga principle: two-thirds and one-third. And insist on a receipt. If a landlord refuses, keep his share of the harvest at your own house or deposit it at the Samiti's stores. Organize volunteer forces, cut branches for lathis, raise banners, pick up your sickles and shout, "We want Tebhaga!" '

From time to time Keshto-da interspersed his speech with slogans which were shouted back by a hundred voices. Occasionally there were questions, such as 'What do we do if the police come?' and 'How can we break the law?' and so on. They became silent once the questions were answered to their satisfaction. The excitement and enthusiasm were infectious. When Keshto-da shouted, 'We'll harvest the rice tomorrow!' everyone roared back, 'We'll harvest the rice tomorrow! We will!'

A few of the jotedars' hirelings were also present at the meeting. These were the ones who had raised the bogey of the law. After Keshto-da's speech, the sharecroppers said, 'Whatever we do is the law, there's no other law. We'll form our committees and set up our own courts. If the jotedars make mischief, we'll teach them justice.'

Dinesh-da spoke next, in the local dialect. 'No use creeping into your shells like tortoises everytime you see a rich man. Start walking with your heads held high. The rich say that we are dancing like whores to the refrains of Tebhaga. What I want to know is, who made whores of us anyway? And having turned us into

AT THE NIGHT MEETING. 19 DECEMBER 1946.

whores, why does it hurt them to see us dance? Let the rich say what they want, we are going to harvest the rice and have the Tebhaga!'

Hearing their innermost feelings expressed in their own language, the people were elated: they clapped loudly, cheered and sat up expectantly, eager to hear what Dinesh-da would say next.

The place began to resound with slogans. 'We want our two thirds, not just half'; 'No rice without a receipt'; 'No interest on rice loans'; 'Remove the harvest to your own homes'; 'Long live the Krishak Saimti'; 'Long live the revolution' and so on. Some of the peasants didn't join in to begin with. As soon as Dinesh-da announced that he would consider those who

LISTENING TO THE SPEECHES.
19 DECEMBER 1946.

THE NIGHT MEETING.
19 DECEMBER 1946.

AN ATTENTIVE FACE.
19 DECEMBER 1946.

WOOD ENGRAVING I

WOOD ENGRAVING II

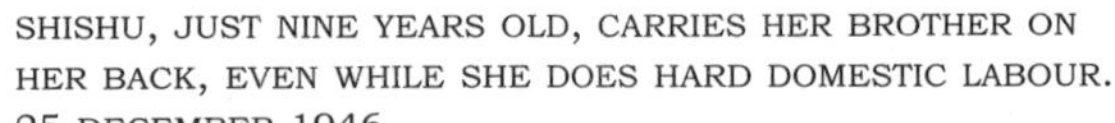

SHISHU, JUST NINE YEARS OLD, CARRIES HER BROTHER ON HER BACK, EVEN WHILE SHE DOES HARD DOMESTIC LABOUR. 25 DECEMBER 1946.

A SCHOOL FOR SHARECROPPERS' AND PEASANTS' CHILDREN. 20 DECEMBER 1946.

kept silent to be the jotedars' stooges, however, everyone, young and old, started shouting slogans with great gusto. The handful of hirelings present had perforce to join in, otherwise they would have been marked out at once, and there's nothing as bad as being identified as a landlord's hirelings at such gatherings, for the jotedar is the peasant's enemy, the country's enemy.

The meeting decided that the harvesting would start the next day and be completed in seven days' time. The various rice fields to be harvested were also decided upon.

After the meeting broke up, the sharecroppers were beaming. Such excitement on every face! Since arriving at this village, there's one word which I have heard frequently: freedom. 'The peasant is winning his freedom,' they say. As I entered the village this morning, a young sharecropper said, 'We are free at last.' And, at night, I heard the same words from young and old alike: they were on their way to freedom. They were not afraid of either the police or the landlord's thugs; they were ready to give their lives, but not their rice; they might die but those who remained would live as free men and women. No one would dare oppress them any more.

YOUNG MAN IN LOINCLOTH.
20 DECEMBER 1946.

FLAGS AND LATHIS AT THE PADDY FIELD.
20 DECEMBER 1946.

at the paddy field 20 · 12 · 46

HARVESTING PADDY.
20 DECEMBER 1946.

Friday, 20 December 1946

The harvesting was to start this morning. Everyone had decided to gather by about nine. We took our flags and went to the field. We were told that people were on their way, but, in the event, they arrived fairly late for they had to have their meal before they came. Once the harvesting started, there would be no time to snatch a bite to eat and by the time it was over it would be very late indeed.

About 150 people had gathered, with virtually everyone carrying a sickle and a lathi. Even children of five or six were carrying sickles or holding up banners.

The red flag was raised in the middle of the field. The boundaries were indicated with flags. The lathis were planted at one spot and everyone trooped into the field with sickles in hand. The air reverberated with slogans. People broke into song, 'Your red flag's your red salute, O

COLLECTIVE HARVESTING. 20 DECEMBER 1946.

peasant.' The rice was harvested to the rhythm of the song. Even the elderly, those whose faces were lined with age, whose teeth were falling out, joined in the singing and chanted the slogans.

They could not even have imagined all this a year ago, for till then both the harvest and the law had belonged to the rich. The sharecropper would slave the year round, growing the paddy; at the end of the year, he would deposit it with the jotedar and spend another long year in suffering and hunger. Now, for the first time, he was free, through unity. He had discovered that he too was strong, that he too had law on his side. Fortified with this newly discovered strength, he was harvesting today and thinking, 'My rights have finally been recognized.' This was the source of his joy.

HARVESTING PADDY.
20 DECEMBER 1946.

WORKING TOGETHER.
20 DECEMBER 1946.

The peasant whose crop was being harvested lived close by. People went in groups to store it for him. The women of his household were watching the harvesting with rapt attention. The red flag was flying over his house. These days the red flag had more auspicious potential than the traditional stalk of plantain and the sacred clay pitcher beside the door.

From naked little children to old men in loincloths, to say nothing of young men clad in brief *gamchhaas*, everyone helped carry the harvest in. A long line of dancing people stretched from the field to the sharecropper's house.

After cutting about four or five *dones* [about 14 kilogrammes] of paddy, people sat down in a large circle for a snack. The man whose

A QUICK BREAK FOR MID-MORNING 'TIFFIN'.
20 DECEMBER 1946.

field was being harvested had brought *muri-murki* or puffed rice to feed the reapers. Everyone ate with great relish though the quantity was small. But then it was decided that there would be no further mid-morning bite from now on. Today's 'snack' had cost seven rupees. Instead, the sharecropper would donate a small sum to the Krishak Samiti funds, and they would all come to work after having eaten their meals at home.

More chanting, flags, drums, songs. Once again everyone entered the field, and the harvesting continued. From a distance it seemed as if a flock of black and white *khanjana* birds was searching for food on a golden sand bank, tails fluttering. Nearly seven *dones* were harvested and stored in sharecropper Jogi Burman's house. During the famine of 1943, Jogi Burman had had part of his land seized by Kailash Adhikari, the local jotedar. This land was recovered today. People left for their homes after

SLOGANS ENLIVEN THE HARVESTING.
20 DECEMBER 1946.

READING *SWADHINATA* AT BADGACHHA.
20 DECEMBER 1946.

the harvesting was over for the day. Everyone was elated, wreathed in smiles, sharecropper and peasant alike. The joy on their faces was like that on the face of a hungry person when he has his first mouthful of food. The long hunger for their rightful share was on its way to being satisfied. This was what had turned today's harvesting into a veritable festival. I had found out from talking to them that they considered Kali Puja their greatest festival. Yet I don't think even Kali Puja had ever occasioned as much joy as today's harvesting.

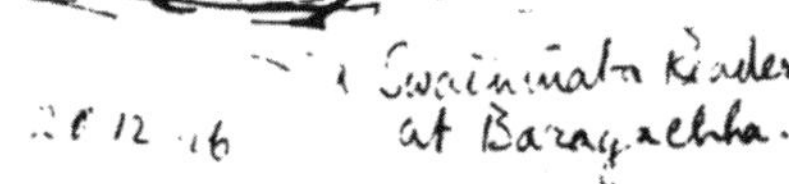

THE *SWADHINATA* IS POPULAR HERE.
20 DECEMBER 1946.

PEASANT LIFE IS HARD, POVERTY-STRICKEN.
21 DECEMBER 1946.

At night, in the camp, I sat down to write, but never got around to it. The sharecroppers arrived in ones and twos, for no special purpose except to chat and exchange stories, mostly about rice harvesting. Apparently Nagen Choudhury, brother of jotedar Kailash Choudhury, had visited the police station to ask for help. The police, it seems, had demanded much more money than expected. And Khoka Thakur had taken real fright; he was rumoured to be coming around soon for a compromise. So the tales went.

In fact, Khoka Thakur did turn up later at night, around ten o'clock, accompanied by a few of his people. He said, 'I'm sorry I tried to stop the drumming in the market square. I was wrong, I admit it. I'll meet your demands. Please enroll me as a member of your Samiti.' The peasants were delighted at this development. 'We've finally managed to cow that ruthless Khoka Thakur. Since we've brought him to heel, the others will fall into line. This is the result of our unity.'

But Khoka Thakur had a trick up his sleeve. As soon as he was made a member of the Samiti he said, 'Someone of my standing must be given an appropriate post in the Association. And since I'm a lot cleverer than you people, you'd better follow my advice. The first thing I advise you all to do is to harvest jotedar Mahatap Miyan's rice crop. Do this tomorrow itself. For if you can only teach him a lesson, all the jotedars are under my control.'

The innocent farmers and sharecroppers gave their assent to this proposal. Afterwards comrades discovered that Mahatap Miyan was not only a member of the Muslim League, but that most of his sharecroppers were Hindu. The few Muslim sharecroppers that he had were skeptical about the prospects of the Tebhaga movement. There was thus the danger of communal strife if the Hindu sharecroppers were to promptly start harvesting the rice. So Panchu and Narayan, two local comrades, warned the peasant elders about the dangers of such a course as soon as they realized what might happen. It was decided that Khoka Thakur's fields would be harvested first, and then Mahatap Miyan's. The programme for 21 December had already been decided upon—the fields of Hafiz, a jotedar, were to be harvested. I went to bed around half past-twelve.

Saturday, 21 December 1946

I've been feeling the cold after arriving in Rangpur. I don't sleep very well because of the cold.

I'd taken my notebook along in the morning in the hope that I would be able to sketch a few vignettes from the life of the sharecroppers. This could not be done. I wanted to sketch the rice being husked, but the women simply would not agree.

I started walking towards the field that was due to be harvested that day. I could see the Kanchenjunga in the distance, against the sky. This was my first view of the mountain. I tried very hard to see if I could make out the details—its undulating

A PROUD TODDLER WITH HIS LATHI.
21 DECEMBER 1946.

HARVESTING RICE.
21 DECEMBER 1946.

undergrowth and trees, the mounds and ravines and a hundred other details. But it just wasn't possible. It was very much like touching a picture drawn on paper—one can't feel any details. The mountain seemed like a picture painted on a flat, smooth sky.

About 50 people had gathered today as well, to harvest the rice. The land belonged to jotedar Hafiz Miyan; his sharecroppers were Qasimuddin and Gelgelo. As on the previous day, there were songs, flags, slogans, all through the harvesting. Today's harvesting looked like a new kind of harvest festival. The same auspicious ceremonials that had marked the Hindu sharecroppers' harvesting yesterday were repeated today for the Muslim sharecroppers. The same preparations, the very same rituals. Those who plough the land and grow crops are neither Hindus nor Muslims—they are farmers.

On the way home, I bought two annas' worth of puffed rice. I had paid only for some *muri*, but what arrived was both *muri and moa*, or puffed rice candy. And the sheer quantity was so astonishing that I asked the comrade who was accompanying me, 'All this for two annas?' He replied, 'But you're a comrade. Naturally they'll give more to a comrade.' The comrade is greatly loved by the children here.

On the way my young sharecropper companion told me about a beautiful local custom. Since my arrival I'd been noticing that the local women draped themselves in a single length of cloth, covering them from chest to knee. Only rarely did I see someone wearing a sari in the manner of our urban women. Nor had I seen anyone covering her head. They have their own way, it seems, of showing respect for their husband's elder brother: by doing up their hair in a bun whenever they have to work in front of their *bhasur*. They don't have to cover their heads in his presence, but they can't speak to him directly. They wear the vermilion mark and conch bangles prescribed for married women, though that custom is fast disappearing—conch bangles are too expensive these days.

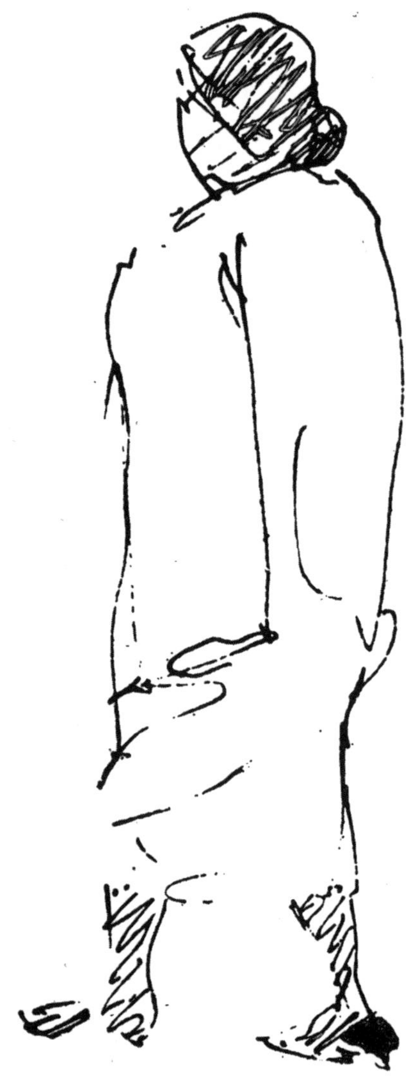

WOMAN DRAPED IN A PIECE OF CLOTH FROM CHEST TO KNEE. 23 DECEMBER 1946.

Widows cut their hair very, very short, much shorter than the men. There's no purdah for them. Nevertheless they carry themselves with considerable diffidence.

Another thing that struck me was that during the few days that I was in Badgachha I hadn't heard the women quarrelling or even arguing loudly. This was quite unusual in small communities, where a few families live in close proximity and know each other very well. Disputes are generally inevitable in such places. I found out on enquiry that quarrels and arguments had been only too common once, but had recently become rare. None of them had pondered why this was happening. When I suggested that the peasant movement was perhaps responsible in some way, everyone agreed that it was very likely. During the course of events, people seemed to have become friendlier with one another. As a result of the movement, men and women sought one another's friendship and company more and more.

LAKHIA.
21 DECEMBER 1946.

In the late afternoon I started out towards Domar. Before leaving, I asked one of the sharecroppers, 'Well, comrade, are you confident that you'll be able to keep the rice?' The answer was prompt, 'We won't give up the rice. We'll sacrifice ourselves but not the rice.' The fiendish jotedars wouldn't get the rice, even with the help of their hired thugs and the police: this was the message I took with me as I left Badgachha. A place which had peasant elders like Mohan-da and Rupkanta-da, sturdy volunteers like Lakhia and Qasimuddin, peasant leaders like Dinesh-da and red flag activists like Narayan and Panchu-da, was bound to wrest victory for its Tebhaga movement.

QASIMUDDIN.
21 DECEMBER 1946.

Sunday, 22 December 1946 (Domar)

Around nine in the morning I heard that Mani Krishna Sen and a sharecropper comrade had reached Domar in an injured condition. Mani-da was organizing the movement from Dimla. The jotedars there had become quite incensed at its success. A Marwari jotedar, having failed to hire hoodlums for the purpose, had gathered some people from his household and attacked Mani-da and the other comrade with a lathi. Mani-da was, at the time, sitting down to meal at local sharecropper Baburi Burman's house. After Mani-da was hit with a lathi, the sharecropper's elderly mother gave the Marwari a good thrashing with a large pestle. Meanwhile, people had started collecting and the Marwari and his household thugs turned tail and ran for their lives.

BABURI BURMAN.
22 DECEMBER 1946.

I went to the Krishak Samiti office and saw Mani-da. He had sustained a nasty scalp wound; blood had seeped through the handkerchief round his head and congealed. The other comrade, Bipin Burman, had also been injured rather badly. The doctor arrived in a little while and dressed their wounds. He said they would recover soon. The Domar market-place was buzzing with talk of the Tebhaga movement. Virtually every stall had a cluster of people before it, huddling in the winter sun. They were all excitedly discussing the same thing—Tebhaga—some supporting it, others criticizing it.

MANI-DA.
22 DECEMBER 1946.

When I got back, I heard that the Badgachha jotedar Nagen Choudhury had asked for help from the Domar police on 20 December in order to prevent the peasants from harvesting his fields. The police had demanded a very large bribe and suggested that he first instigate some serious trouble in Badgachha.

The students were very worked up about the attack on Mani-da. They had decided to hold a protest rally against the murderous Marwari that afternoon.

It was soon after midday that I set out in a bullock cart for Dimla. Between the beautiful scenery around me and the jolting bullock cart, I trundled along till we reached Gayabadi in the evening. I was to stay the night with comrade Harikanta Sarkar. The first thing I learnt was that the most popular slogans with the local peasants were, 'We want the murderous Marwari's head', and 'Blood for blood'. Harikanta-da and the other comrades had managed to restrain them with considerable difficulty.

The preparations for the rice harvesting were going full steam ahead. The Marwari jotedars had been greatly frightened over the incident in which Mani-da was attacked. Many were sending their women folk to the city.

The peasants were now very united. The Marwaris hadn't made a dent in their unity in spite of spending huge sums of money. 'First we harvest the rice and remove it to our own homes. Then we negotiate.'

This was my first meeting with Harikanta-da. He was a powerfully built man with a bright, lively face and eyes sparkling with vitality. Though about 40 years old, he was as restless and excitable in his conversation as any of us. The local jotedars were prepared to pay a lakh of rupees for Harikanta-da's head—provided, of course, that their own heads were safe. However, as they seem unable to manage both jobs simultaneously, they're keeping themselves busy saving their own heads.

I heard the real story about the attack on Mani Sen by the jotedar's strong-arm boys from Harikanta-da and comrade Mohi Bagchi. The information I had received in Domar had been inaccurate. As Mani-da was preparing to sit down for his midday meal at Baburi Burman's house on 20 December, jotedar Koramal came there with about a dozen people, mostly Bhutiyas and some guards, and raised a clamour. When Mani-da, alerted by the noise, went up to them, Koramal charged him, 'Are you the man who's inciting the sharecroppers?' and forthwith struck him on the head with a lathi. At this comrade Bipin Burman attacked Koramal with a small staff, but he had to fall back before Koramal's hired thugs. It was at this moment that Baburi's old mother, the only other person in the house, picked up a husking pestle and hit Koramal. She was struck down by Koramal's thugs, who then ran away and hid in a nearby shed which belonged to Koramal. Meanwhile, people had started gathering on receiving news of what had happened. Koramal, unnerved by this, started firing in the air to scare them away. He went on thus firing continuously till the evening, when he could slink home under the cover of darkness. (Koramal had brought two guns with him.) Mani Sen and Bipin Burman had both received serious injuries to their heads, as well as on other parts of their bodies.

MOHI-DA.
25 DECEMBER 1946.

A BULLOCK CART, COMMON MEANS OF TRANSPORT.

Monday, 23 December 1946

Wherever I have been among the peasants, I have noticed the common people's deep contempt for the Congress and the Muslim League. Hindu sharecroppers consider the Congress their enemy. Muslim sharecroppers have similar feelings about the Muslim League. They consider the Congress and the League the dens of the landlords. In Badgachha, an elderly farmer said to me, 'For the past 50 or 60 years, the Congress people have been telling us that they are serving our interests, and yet I've never seen them doing anything for us. Now we don't want to have anything to do with the Congress Party. The comrades are here, and have started fighting for us. They have shown us the way to survive. They are the only ones who are sympathetic towards us, our real friends.' The Congress supporters in the cities would not believe me. And if they did, their stock answer would be—such men are traitors and Communist touts. But one has only to confront these exploited and yet heroic peasants and examine one's conscience to find out who the real touts, knowing or unknowing, are.

The pregnant earth is giving birth to new life today. The birth pangs are immense, but so are the expectations and possibilities. Are the general supporters of the Congress and the League going to remain blind to these new possibilities and not welcome them?

I didn't go out this morning. In the afternoon I had a short nap. Later, I went to Harikanta-da's house. Two peasant activists turned up while I was there. One was a tall, powerfully built man, with a formidable lathi. The first thing he asked was, 'Have you heard about Mani Sen?' When we said yes, he heaved a huge sigh and said, 'Oh, if only I had been around. I'd have soon sorted the Marwari out. Give me permission even now, and I'll fix those bastards.'

JAMSHED ALI.

This peasant activist's name was Jamshed Ali. The local comrades told me an amusing story about him.

Each time he sees a Party worker passing his house, he drops whatever he's doing, rushes out and asks, 'What news of the Party, comrade?' On being told that the Party's work is getting on fine everywhere, and that the struggle is going ahead, he exclaims, 'That's a relief!' Then he goes round from house to house in the neighbourhood declaring, 'Who's going to stop the Party now? We'll blast the League apart. All their loud talk isn't going to work around here, I can tell you'; and so on.

I found out that his anger against the League is due to the fact that the local jotedars are members of the League. They are using the cover of the Muslim League to exploit the poor peasants. Jamshed Ali is a sharecropper.

A little after sundown, some people could be heard shouting slogans: 'Victory to the Krishak Samiti', and 'Not half, we want our two-thirds.' It sounded as though hardly two or three people were shouting. A comrade who was present said, 'This sort of slogan-shouting is very common in these parts. People just shout such things out of sheer exuberance, from time to time.'

Quite a few people gathered in Harikanta-da's drawing room at night. In the ensuing discussion, I heard a tragic story about a sharecropper.

His name was Khadu Burman, and he lived in a village called Nautera Tepa in Dimla Thana. He had taken a plot of 20 *dones* on

SHARECROPPERS AT HARIKANTA-DA'S HOUSE.
24 DECEMBER 1946.

loan from jotedar Siraj Miyan on a *chukani* deal by which the sharecropper repays the jotedar almost five times the original amount. The harvest was poor one year, and Khadu's share was too small to feed his family for a year. So he had to sell his plough and bullocks and managed to live off the proceeds for a while. But the jotedar's accounts showed huge arrears on Khadu's part, and he seized Khadu's land in repayment of his loan. After much pleading with Siraj Miyan, Khadu managed to make a fresh deal that allowed him to start farming the same land, but as a sharecropper. He had to borrow the plough and bullocks from the jotedar this time. Once the crop was harvested, it was taken straight to the landlord's granary, where it was divided after the landlord had kept aside the seed grain. The division was made on the traditional sharecropping basis. After this the landlord made various deductions from Khadu's share. These included one *done* as payment for the watchman, a *done* and a half for his office clerk, a *done* for every 20 for those who weighed the paddy, a *done* as service charge for storing the grain in his granary. The paddy taken on loan was recovered at the rate of one and a half times. The jotedar showed arrears still outstanding after he had seized all the paddy in Khadu's share. Khadu's pleading was in vain. After all this, the jotedar refused a further loan saying that there was no way Khadu could repay it; and took his plough and bullocks back. Khadu became a day labourer. In a short while, the family was forced to leave. They went to live in Gomna village, where he died of starvation during the last famine.

TOGRU MOHAMMED.
23 DECEMBER 1946.

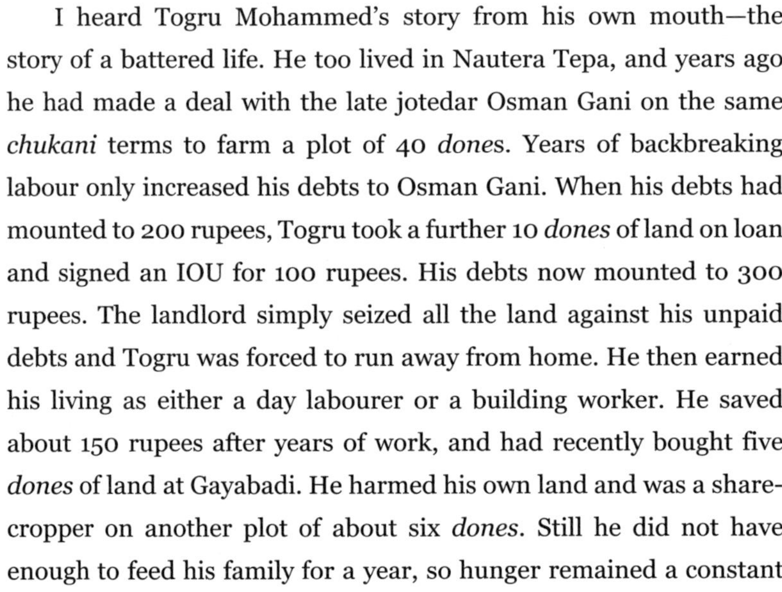

I heard Togru Mohammed's story from his own mouth—the story of a battered life. He too lived in Nautera Tepa, and years ago he had made a deal with the late jotedar Osman Gani on the same *chukani* terms to farm a plot of 40 *dones*. Years of backbreaking labour only increased his debts to Osman Gani. When his debts had mounted to 200 rupees, Togru took a further 10 *dones* of land on loan and signed an IOU for 100 rupees. His debts now mounted to 300 rupees. The landlord simply seized all the land against his unpaid debts and Togru was forced to run away from home. He then earned his living as either a day labourer or a building worker. He saved about 150 rupees after years of work, and had recently bought five *dones* of land at Gayabadi. He harmed his own land and was a sharecropper on another plot of about six *dones*. Still he did not have enough to feed his family for a year, so hunger remained a constant

WOOD ENGRAVING III

companion. How could a family of 10 survive on the produce of such a small plot of land?

Now an old man of 60 with a flowing white beard, Togru Mohammed's face is lined and scarred by the years of unjust exploitation he has suffered. At the mere mention of jotedars he breaks into a roar; he seems to swell and spit in rage, like an angered cobra. His eyes burning with vengeance he yells, 'We must have Tebhaga! I'll rid this world of jotedars!' These are words that come from the hearts of both Hindu and Muslim peasants. This country is full of Togru Mohammeds and Khadu Burmans. Each day has added to the burden of their losses till they have been pushed to a point where they have no option but to rise in protest. So now Jamshed Ali carried a large lathi, and Togru Mohammed's eyes burn with revenge and everyone's voice carried the same message, 'Run, jotedar, run.'

Tuesday, 24 December 1946

Today, the field of share-cropper Shakruddin was harvested. Shakruddin lives in Dimla. He works on the land of jotedar Majidullah Sircar who lives in Uttar Titpara village. In all, Majidullah's land covers almost a village and a half.

Having heard that Shakruddin was planning to harvest his crop today, Majidullah arrived at his house at half-past seven in the morning, accompanied by another landlord. He spent the next four hours trying his best to dissuade Shakruddin. What Majidullah said was something to this effect: 'If you harvest my rice and remove it to your own granary, the other sharecroppers will follow your example. So my request to you is, please don't take the rice to your granary. I'll do everything to make your life easy for you.' Shakruddin flatly refused, which made the landlord angry. He tried to frighten him by saying, 'The next time things are difficult, I'll make sure you don't get a loan. And next year I won't let you in on my land.' Shakruddin remained quite unmoved by these threats. Finally, the jotedar took him aside and offered him 50 rupees. Shakruddin turned this down with the contempt it deserved, and told the landlord that he was not the type to let down the people with whom he had cast in his lot. The jotedar left with the threat, 'Wait till I get my chance!'

SHAKRUDDIN.
24 DECEMBER 1946.

This is Shakruddin, a sharecropper. The fence around his house is falling down, the thatch on his roof is rotting, his clothes are torn and ragged, his women folk can't come out in public because they have nothing to clothe themselves with. They can't afford two meals a day for most of the year. But the man's determination is remarkable. The landlord offered him every kind of inducement, pleaded with him, but Shakruddin just wouldn't break his word. I thought of our selfless national leader Pandit Nehru. Whenever a purse of a lakh of rupees is given to him, he seems to forget all about his promises to hang the blackmarketeers from the nearest lamppost. Whenever there is talk of weighing him against gold or silver, he tends to forget his commitment to oust our native princes. But never mind all that. For Panditji will always be adored as a selfless man; after all, he is a great leader. And Shakruddin—he will always be branded either a tout of the traitorous Communists or a peasant thug for he won't succumb to bribes and insists on getting his rights.

About 30 volunteers started harvesting the rice with sickles. In a little while, Majidullah's son arrived and began to abuse them. The volunteers had no time to listen to him; they calmly carried on with

DISCUSSING TEBHAGA.
24 DECEMBER 1946.

24 12 46

their job. Suddenly, a friend of the jotedar started exclaiming, 'What injustice in God's Kingdom! How dare you harvest the rice using brute force! God will certainly punish you people for this.' There were disdainful smiles on some faces—the devil quoting scriptures! The jotedar and his cronies went away disappointed.

The rice was stored in the sharecropper's house by long lines of reapers chanting slogans.

Late in the afternoon, about 150 volunteers armed with lathis went to the market at Satibadi to hold a meeting. They gathered at one spot after circling the market. Vendors left their stalls and the entire market crowd joined the meeting. Harikanta-da and Mohi Bagchi spoke about Tebhaga. Thy asked the people to assert the triumph of Tebhaga by revenging the vicious attack on Mani Sen by the jotedar. 'The murderous jotedar must be punished' was the principal slogan of the meeting. Afterwards, the volunteers collected rice, vegetables and other things from the people at the market.

On the way back from the market, I overheard a conversation between two persons. One was saying to the other, 'If I take part in the movement this year, the jotedar won't give me any land next year. Where do I get my land, then?' The other man asked, 'But don't you have your plough and pair of bullocks?' The first man replied, 'Yes, I do.' Promptly the other man said, 'That's all you need. The landlord can't physically remove the land, can he?' I realized that the demand of 'land to the tiller' was being born in the womb of the Tebhaga movement.

There are two slogans which are often heard in Dimla these days, one from the landlords and the other from the sharecroppers. The

SOMNATH HORE

PROCESSIONISTS GATHER BEFORE MARCHING TO SATIBADI MARKET.
24 DECEMBER 1946.

A PROCESSION BOUND FOR SATIBADI IN PROTEST AGAINST JOTEDAR TYRANNY.
24 DECEMBER 1946.

WOOD ENGRAVING IV

landlords say amongst themselves, 'We want the *kainyas'* (Marwaris') heads.' Later that night I heard from a comrade about the laments of three jotedars. Apparently, he had met the three jotedars after meeting at Satibadi market. They were Umesh Sarkar from Khadibadi, Mahesh Sarkar and Ichhamuddi of Gayabadi. In the course of conversation, Mahesh Sarkar told him sadly, 'You know, we don't keep track of what the sharecroppers are doing; we often don't have time to inspect our land. And each year they remove nearly 90 per cent of the crop without our knowledge. Only the remaining 10 per cent reaches our granaries. Our share's barely half of that. Now the sharecroppers are talking about Tebhaga. Well, let's have Tebhaga then, we don't mind. But for God's sake don't let's spoil the old master-servant relationship. The way you people are inciting our subjects, they don't even obey us or bother to listen to us any more. Please don't ruin the master-servant relationship.' Quite obviously, our local tinpot princelings can feel the ground opening up under their feet.

A pleasant note: the word 'comrade' is very popular in these parts. Anyone and everyone will greet you as 'comrade' and everyone responds to it. From children of four to old people of 70 they call us comrade and that is what we call them in return.

And the lathi: meetings, processions, harvesting, wherever one goes, one must have a lathi. No one pays attention to you if you don't have one.

PEASANT HUTS.
24 DECEMBER 1946.

Wednesday, 25 December 1946

I was sketching a peasant hut in Harikanta-da's house when the police arrived—a sergeant and a constable. 'We want Harikanta-babu?' 'Why?' 'Don't you know, the inspector wants to see him.' 'Well, where is the inspector?' 'He's in the car outside.' After I told them that Harikanta-babu was not in, the pair fidgeted for a while and then left.

I heard later that Harikanta-babu had met this lot. The officer had threatened to arrest him on charges of looting jotedar Koramal's granary. Of course Harikanta-da paid not a jot of attention to this nonsense—the man was out of uniform, had no warrant and, above all, was travelling in Koramal's car as if he was on his way to his in-laws. Meeting Harikanta-babu on the road, he had said, 'I've got an unpleasant piece of news to give you. I have to arrest you.'

Everyone knew that the inspector was lining his pocket. 'Koramal goes and attacks someone and this man comes to arrest Harikanta Sarkar on charges of looting Koramal's granary! They must think we people are fools.' This was the comment I heard everywhere I went. And the rumour was that the inspector had said that there were similar charges of looting against 30 or 35 people. (Later we learnt that he was merely a sergeant from Dimla and not an inspector.)

I heard from comrade Mohi that apparently Koramal had earlier asked the inspector from Dimla Police Thana to stop the harvesting. This man had told Koramal that they didn't have the authority to do so, but, if he could organize some kind of fracas and build a case on that, then they could find a way to help him out.

A few days later, Mani Krishna Sen was attacked. And today, there was this threat of arrest.

The ordinary peasants fear that the jotedars and the corrupt officials are conspiring to arrest the leaders of the movement and keep them in the lock-up for a few days, so that the jotedars can use the opportunity to harvest the rice and remove it to their own granaries. Obviously, the real motive is to simultaneously harvest the rice and break the movement, for it is quite clear that the charges will not stick. So the peasants have decided that they will prevent the arrests of their leaders and harvest the rice as soon as possible, storing it in their own houses. Then they will wait and see how far the legal games go.

WOOD ENGRAVING V

Preparations were going on at full speed for non-stop harvesting. The sharecroppers seemed absolutely determined to overcome every obstacle and make a success of the movement.

Today, the Khadibadi landlord Umesh Sarkar's rice was harvested. About 50 volunteers went to the fields armed with lathis. In all, seven sharecroppers' rice has been harvested.

The harvesting is in full swing all around. Generally, the volunteers begin the harvesting of a sharecropper's rice and remove it to his granary. From the next day onwards, the sharecropper does the

WOOD ENGRAVING VI

harvesting on his own. Where there is a possibility of an attack by the jotedars' men, the volunteers complete the task of storing the grain as an added source of protection.

I ate with comrade Jatin in the afternoon. Rice, dal and fritters of small fish and brinjal.

Since coming to these parts I've noticed that the people here eat their rice with just dal and a piece of fried vegetable or fish. It was the same at Badgachha. There don't seem to be as many vegetables available here as we have in our district. And the same goes for fish. In any case, the poor sharecropper tends to think of rice and dal, or rice and some fried vegetable, as enough of a meal. It's remarkable that people can live on so little protein and vitamin. Of course, the local rice is of fine quality and is rich in vitamins. Presumably that is what nourishes them somewhat. The quality of cooking is very poor.

We ate *saoda* at Harikanta-da's elder brother's house at night. *Saoda* is the curd, *khoi* (parched rice) and *chida* (flattened rice) that married daughters bring with them when they visit their parents. There was plenty of it. After the meal I learnt that this *saoda* had come from the house of jotedar Umesh Sarkar whose crop had

THRESHING GRAIN.
25 DECEMBER 1946.

WOMAN AND CHILD.
25 DECEMBER 1946.

been harvested that day. Harikanta-da's niece is married to Umesh Sarkar's son.

Umesh Sarkar had tried to use this relationship to influence Harikanta-da and wangle an exemption from Tebhaga. He was doomed to disappointment. A comrade joked, 'He must be trying to cool us down with this curd on a winter's night. But we won't cool off!'

I had no inclination to have dinner after eating *saoda*. But I had to, for they had cooked 'mutton-rice'. It's only when I sat down to the meal that I realized what 'mutton-rice' was—it was mutton curry and rice.

Harikanta-da, Abani Bagchi and some other comrades left for a meeting after finishing their meal. Early next morning Koramal Daga's field were to be extensively harvested. The meeting had been called to co-ordinate the preparations for it.

A comrade returned from Teparhat with the report that the landlords were carrying out a campaign to the effect that Harikanta-da and the other comrades were government agents. The jotedars are obviously in a state of panic.

In one of the rooms a young sharecropper is singing:

The sun brings glory to the day,
To the night, the moon.
A ploughman's glory is his ploughing
And land's is in its paddy.

He has a sweet voice.

Thursday, 26 December 1946

I made a sketch of Baburi Burman's mother today. The old lady must be over seventy. This is the woman who had struck Koramal Daga with a pestle. 'Weren't you at all scared when you hit the Marwari?' I asked. 'Scared? Why? He was beating up my kids, so I beat him up.'

Her teeth have fallen out, so she finds it hard to speak clearly. Her eyes have sunk into folds of wrinkled flesh, here eyesight is poor. She can hear only with great difficulty, and she can hardly walk. Yet this old woman opposed the landlord's bullying with a pestle in her hands. After lifetimes of oppression and humiliation, the peasant is finally standing upright.

JATIN.
26 DECEMBER 1946.

On the way back, the comrade accompanying me pointed out a house and said, 'That's Sarada Mohan Roy's house. He has sided with the Marwaris. He's a Congressman.' A Congressman is synonymous with an enemy.

In the afternoon I heard that that very morning the biggest jotedar from Khaga had summoned some of his sharecroppers and administered a severe beating to two or three of them. Their crime—joining the Krishak Samiti, and refusing to store the harvested grain in his granary. The local peasants and sharecroppers are absolutely wild with rage. They called a meeting on their own, and are demanding that the 'murderous jotedar' be brought to trial!

I made a sketch of comrade Jatin, a very enthusiastic and hard-working activist in the Krishak Samiti. He is a member of the Communist Party. As a sharecropper he barely manages to feed his family. Not older than 24, he is quite fearless and daring. His lathi is his favourite possession.

The sketch alongside is of Durgacharan Sarkar, Harikannta-da's elder brother. He is over 50, and calls us 'comrade', which is how we also address him. I've noticed that he enjoys reading the daily *Swadhinata* whenever he can. He absorbs the news on Tebhaga in one breath, and then starts a discussion with the sharecroppers and peasants who happen to be around. He hates the *Ananda Bazar Patrika* because it's apparently an anti-Tebhaga paper.

The volunteers have harvested fields in Dimla, north Gayabadi and some other places today, and removed the harvest to the sharecroppers' homes. Besides, the sharecroppers are themselves carrying on the work in all the fields where the volunteers had already initiated collective harvesting.

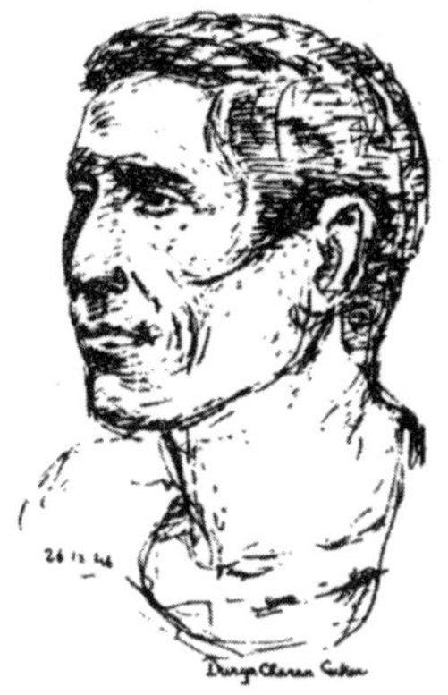

DURGACHARAN SARKAR. 26 DECEMBER 1946.

Comrade Harikanta Sarkar is himself a fairly important jotedar, his land stretching to almost a village and a half. Today his tenant Beechiram Adhikari and sharecropper Rabiram's wife (from the village Nautera Tepa) delivered Harikanta his share of the crop. It goes without saying that the division was on the Tebhaga basis.

At nearly nine at night, a supporter of the Krishak Samiti, a 65-year-old man named Nilkanta Panchayet, arrived with a friend. They were looking for Harikanta-da. They had an important message for him. Apparently, Sarada Mohan Roy, whose name I've mentioned earlier, was now saying that he too was a poor man and was going to side with the poor. The peasants had boycotted him out of a misunderstanding—he had never been on the side of the rich, though he had visited them from time to time out of necessity. But now, if he was made a member of the Krishak Samiti, he would fight for Tebhaga harder than anyone else, against the rich. One of those present said, 'So he realizes the strength of the poor once they stand united!'

It was decided that if Sarada-babu was truly repentant, he would have to prove it by abiding by the judgment of the entire community. Just approaching Harikanta-babu alone was not enough. Harikanta-babu was of the same opinion.

This Sarada-babu used to be a petty trader by profession. He made some money during the war years by acting as a middleman for the Marwaris, and by dealing in the blackmarket. He bought some land with this money and in the process became a small jotedar. From the very beginning he had opposed the Tebhaga movement and hobnobbed openly with Marwaris. It was rumoured that Sarada-babu had been part of Koramal Daga's gang when he attacked Mani Sen in Baburi's house. It was after this event that the local population had boycotted him to express their anger. Within a few days Sarada-babu had started begging for acceptance.

At night, a peasant comrade sang for us. I could see for myself tonight how a new culture was taking root in the ordinary man's life through the activities of the Communist Party. The comrade first sang one of our peasant songs and followed this up with an old folk song from Rangpur, '*Dhenar badhua tui*' ('Oh you bride of Dhena!'), which drew little response from the audience. He then sang '*Dukher rater ghore tamasa bhedi*' ('Piercing the grim darkness of our night of grief') and the entire audience kept time with him. Soon the elderly Nilkanta Panchayet and his equally elderly companion Durga-babu were humming along. After this, one patriotic song followed another and the entire audience, young and old, joined in. They asked for the words that they could not comprehend to be explained, and then sang them again. The older listeners nodded delightedly and said, 'Wonderful', requesting more of the same. These were songs on the elections and voting, on the peasants' daily requirements—cooking oil, salt, fuel—and more patriotic songs. I realized for the first time that those songs which had brought a momentary thrill to our lives had now become part of the culture of everyday life.

Friday, 27 December 1946

I was to leave for Domar last night but the trip had to be cancelled because of lack of transport.

There's an oppressive atmosphere about the harvesting now. The jotedars have banded together and started a war of nerves with the peasants. They've tried terrorizing, spreading rumours, bribing and using the bought-off police in order to bring harvesting to a halt. And on a purely temporary basis they've had some limited success. Though some sharecroppers are still harvesting the crop and storing it, the majority are carefully waiting and watching developments, especially in the areas where the movement is very new. Nevertheless, the landords' persecution is causing great resentment amongst the peasantry. We heard something about how people were reacting to yesterday's incident, when Bhedu Miyan beat up three of his sharecroppers. This morning at Khagakhadibadi, Bhedu Miyan's major domo Tasleem ordered the Muslim sharecroppers to harvest the crop and remove it all to the jotedar's granary. The sharecroppers told him flatly, 'It's our rice, we'll harvest it when we like.' When Tasleem attempted to say something further, they became livid with anger and started shouting, 'Smash the scoundrel!' Tasleem had to take off his shoes and run for his life. Some of the other jotedars have threatened to bring in the Gurkhas, Bhutiyas, additional police from 18 stations and what-have-you. The net result has been—the peasants are becoming more and more united, defying the jotedars with meetings and processions at weekly markets. The peasants are steadily losing their wait-and-see attitude.

This morning Umesh Sarkar ordered one of his sharecroppers to harvest the rice and remove it to his granary. He threatened to evict the man if he reused to obey, and the sharecropper initially lost his nerve. But once he saw the lathi-wielding volunteers on their way to the market in the afternoon, his spirits revived.

'MAMU'—RAMPRASAD BURMAN. 27 DECEMBER 1946.

The peasants are preparing for large-scale harvesting of the richer jotedars' fields. Already fields owned by most of the big land-owners have been harvested. However, it will take some time to gather momentum.

I sketched some of the leaders of the sharecroppers' movement of 1940 this morning. The 65-year-old 'Mamu', Ramprasad Burman, was an enthusiastic activist in that movement. His enthusiasm remains as strong as ever. This afternoon he set out for the village market at Khaga, lathi in hand, to join in the demonstration against the landlords and their oppression. I said, 'You're an elderly man. If the thugs attack you, do you think you'll be able to defend yourself with that lathi?' He answered, 'Well, even if I can't break their bones, I can give them a few bruises, can't I?' When I asked whether he felt Tebaga would be a success he said, 'I've fought in the past, I'm fighting now, and I'll fight in the future. If we keep up the struggle, we're bound to succeed.'

HARENDRA BURMAN.
27 DECEMBER 1946.

Three of this old man's nephews had taken an active part in the previous struggle. One of them, Harendra, had even been interned. Harendra is playing a leading role in the present struggle as well.

I did a sketch of Din Dayal, a resident of their locality. It's very reassuring to look at Din Dayal's smiling face. Two men had been known activist leaders in the Dimla area during the movement of 1940. One was Kalachand and the other this very same Din Dayal. Kalachand still carries the scar from a jotedar's pike on the right side of his chest. Both men have unbounded courage. They are the first to volunteer for any and every task. They entered the political struggle as ordinary peasants and that is the reason why the people of the village trust them implicitly. They too were interned during the 1940 movement.

DIN DAYAL.
27 DECEMBER 1946.

I was returning from Din Dayal's house accompanied by some volunteers, when we met another volunteer going the same way. He fell in with us. He didn't have a lathi and was warned,

KALACHAND.
27 DECEMBER 1946.

'Cut yourself a lathi and then walk with us. You should carry one.' Having told him this, they cut off a branch from a *kul* tree, and gave it to him for a lathi.

I heard another slogan, 'Make *khapad* and kill the swine.' *Khapad* is their word for a pike. The local wild boars often come out of the neighbouring forest and cause extensive damage in the rice fields. But recently the peasants have realized that the jotedars cause even more damage than the boars, since it is their persecution that usually drives the sharecropper to starvation. Hence the slogan.

As we passed through a neighbourhood, a four-year-old boy saw with us and spontaneously broke out with a slogan, 'Vote for Harikanta.'

It's amusing that whenever we've walked through a neighbourhood, both men and women have stared intently for a while, before coming to the conclusion that we're 'comrades'. They ask, 'You're comrades, aren't you?' Then follow the various queries: 'Has the Tebhaga law been passed?', 'Do you think we'll win this struggle?', and so on. 'Comorade' for comrade, 'rain' for *ain* (law) and 'allee' for rally are in common usage here.

Today the fields belonging to Pyari Mohan Sarkar, a big jotedar, were harvested by the volunteers and the crops taken to the sharecropper's house. Many sharecroppers were waiting to see whether Pyari-babu's crops would be harvested at all. After today's work, they have gained fresh courage.

At night I heard that Sarada-babu had gone through a public trial. He had been able to establish that he had not taken part in the attack on Mani Sen. He has been made a member of the Krishak

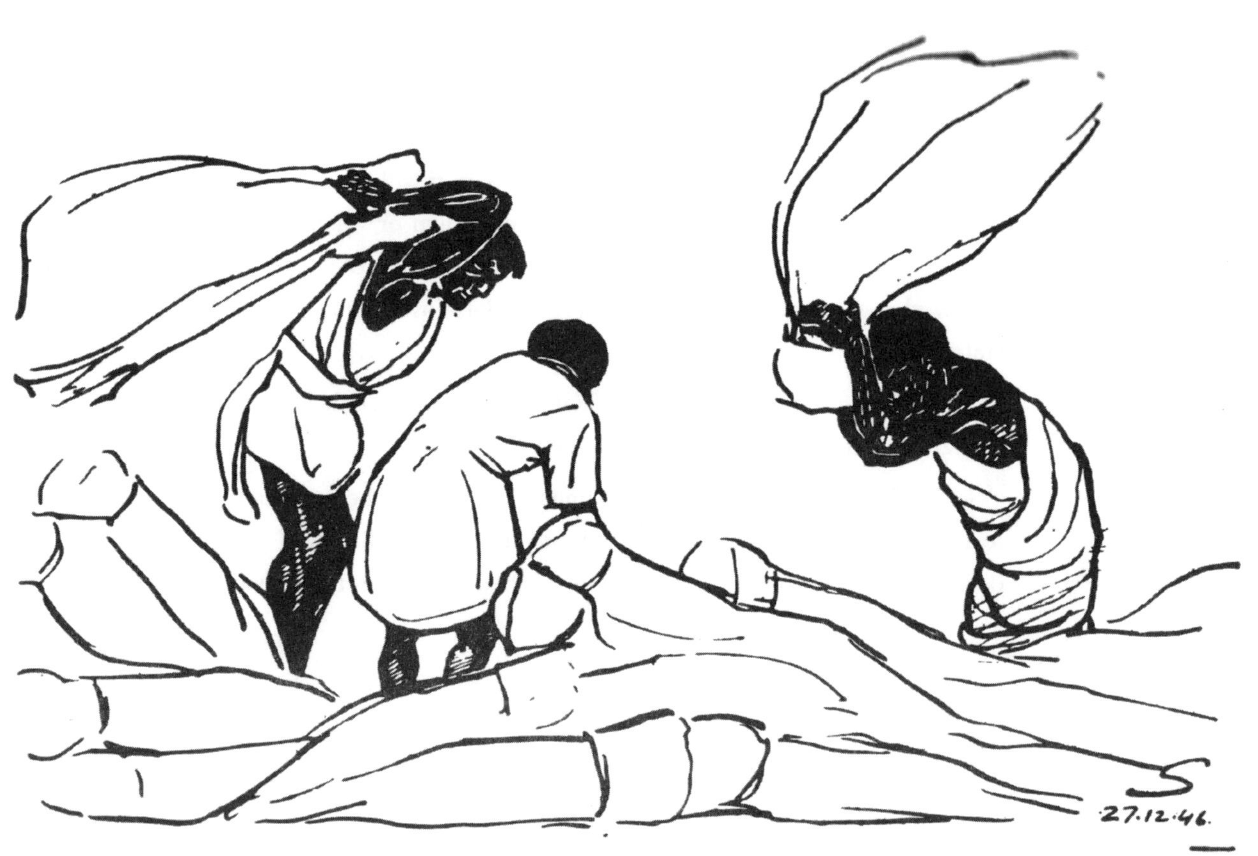

THRESHING RICE.
27 DECEMBER 1946.

Samiti, and has sworn an oath that he will stand by the peasants, work for their benefit and have nothing to do with Marwaris in the future.

The husband of Harikanta-da's niece arrived at night. One of the anti-Tebhaga jotedars, the man had a pathetic expression and a soft tone: 'Whether the sharecroppers take half or two-thirds, why don't they store the rice in our granaries? They don't have any storage space to speak of. Where on earth will they keep it? The rice will either rot or be stolen it it's left lying in the open. Who'll be responsible then?' Harikanta-da reassured him, 'The Samiti will look after the rice. There's no fear whatsoever of its being stolen or wasted. And the rice will be stored by the sharecroppers.' One look at the nephew-in-law showed that he was more perturbed than relieved by this statement.

Mohi Bagchi, Harikanta-da, and Jatin left at around half-past ten at night to attend a closed-door meeting.

The driver of the bullock-cart came to tell me that he was ready to leave. I was going to Domar, I didn't leave immediately. I had decided to leave around midnight and reached Domar around dawn. I went to sleep.

Saturday, 28 December 1946

I got on the bullock-cart around two o'clock this morning. The cart was strewn with straw inside and I spread my bedding on it. I'd imagined that I would be very cold, but I wasn't, as the cart was tightly and heavily covered.

The journey from Domar to Dimla had been most uncomfortable. The oxen had been rather weak and the driver inexperienced; as a result, I had been tossed about until I'd felt quite sick. The journey was much smoother this time, mainly because the driver knew the roads well and could handle his oxen.

I'd doze for a while, gradually fall deeply asleep, then suddenly wake up hearing the rippling of a stream. Just two people journeying through the semi-darkness, under a wide sky, drawn along by two dumb animals—but it did not feel as if we were being borne on their backs: rather, that they were our own legs, our one resource, and would draw us from one end of the earth to the other in this manner. We would crest a rise at times, enter a deep forest at others, or plunge through the wide open heart of the fields. Suddenly the sheer muslin of a flowing stream would appear, so fine that one could fold it in one's hand. As we entered it, such a wild gurgling and splashing! In the deep solitude its murmuring swelled as if, in conversation with a dear friend; it knew that there was no one in the vast velvet darkness to oppose its passion.

I'd see through sleep-heavy eyes that both of us kept dozing off while the oxen continued to pull us on our way. They seemed familiar with every speck of sand on the long road. It seemed as if they could finish the journey even if they became blind, as though the specks of sand, which spoke to their feet as they stepped along, would direct them.

Between night's end and break of day, I saw the eastern sky which we had left behind us transformed into a wondrous vision. Many a time in my life have I seen such vistas and wondered: how does this come about, how does such beauty happen? It seemed as though every atom, every particle of the wide world was rushing in one direction under a ceaseless magnetic pull. No one, and nothing was outside this flow. I think this motion, this constant flow, is the life of a picture. This is why pictures, whether drawn on the earth itself or on a piece of paper, can never lack that dynamism.

On reaching Domar I heard that there had been a major confrontation between the jotedar and his sharecroppers, at a village called Hansaraj. On 25 December, comrade Panchu Turi, with about 60 volunteers, was harvesting a sharecropper's rice, when the tyrannical zamindar of Sonarai arrived with nearly a hundred men, including his relatives, armed with rifles, to stop the harvesting. Seeing the daunting expressions on the volunteers' faces, they kept their distance and started shouting at them, 'We want Panchu! We want Panchu's head!' Meanwhile, word had reached the nearby villages of Dugdugi and Badgachha that Panchu had been surrounded by an armed jotedar and his gun-toting henchmen, and hundreds of peasants armed with lathis turned up to rescue Panchu from their hated enemy. One look at them and the jotedar and his men turned tail.

Their hasty retreat seems to have upset the younger sharecroppers greatly. They had been spoiling for a fight and had carried large stones to use against the jotedars' bullets. But the thugs had run away! They were intensely disappointed.

This is the face of the peasant arisen. They are all here—Madhu, Ledhu, Togru, Rupkanta, Mohan-da, Chati Miyan; with their lathis and sickles they harvest the crops as well as resist the thugs.

Peasants of Domar and Dimla, I felicitate you. The red glow of the new sun shines on your faces. Your fields are darkly stained with blood. You will never surrender the vast golden paddy fields that you have nurtured with drops of your own blood. This I have seen and felt, this is my conviction. Once again, I offer you my congratulations.